# SINGING
## WITHOUT STRAINING THE VOICE

## Elizabeth Cooper

First published in 2012 by

Tomahawk Press
PO Box 1236
Sheffield S11 7XU
England
www.tomahawkpress.com

© Elizabeth Cooper 2012

The right of Elizabeth Cooper to be identified as the author of this work is hereby asserted in accordance with the Copyright, Designs and Patents Act 1988.
All rights reserved. No part of this publication may be reproduced or transmitted in any form or by any means, electronic or mechanical, including photocopy, recording, or other information retrieval system, without permission in writing from the publisher.

ISBN 13: 978-0-9566834-1-0

# Foreword

It is an enormous pleasure and privilege to write this foreword to Elizabeth's booklet on singing technique. Elizabeth is one of those rare, inspirational human beings whose talent and generosity profoundly influence the lives of many others. Her musicianship is as exceptional as her ability to convey her immense knowledge to pupils of all ages and backgrounds.

I began my vocal studies with Elizabeth in 1967 when I was sixteen years old and a pupil at Surbiton High School in Surrey.

At that time, Elizabeth was Professor of Singing in the Junior Department of the Royal Academy of Music as well as being my music teacher at school and it is entirely thanks to her that I was awarded five terms of musical education at the Junior Academy in January 1968.

I have used Elizabeth's technique every day since then

– firstly as her pupil at the RAM; then as student of Constance Shacklock at the senior Academy; and finally as a successful professional singer.

I am still singing all over the world forty four years later, which is testament to the fact that Elizabeth's technique works. I am now passing this knowledge on to young people at the National Opera Studio in London, thus continuing a long line of teaching that goes back into the early 19th century.

As a young woman, Elizabeth was a renowned professional singer of tremendous skill - she was a regular broadcaster on BBC radio and much admired for her bel canto technique and expertise in French repertoire. Unfortunately, family circumstances obliged her to forgo an international singing career and take up teaching instead.

Whilst this was undoubtedly a terrible sacrifice for Elizabeth, it was a stroke of great good fortune for

every one of her subsequent pupils. Not only has Elizabeth trained professional and amateur singers for over 70 years, but she has also taught violin, piano, recorder, aural and theory to the highest level.

In addition to this, Elizabeth is a published composer of significant repute.

Elizabeth is a remarkable teacher, musician and human being. Her booklet will be of inestimable value to singers of all standards – it is clearly explained and covers all the essential elements of vocal technique. Whether you are in a choir or aspire to become a professional soloist, this booklet will help you sing to the best of your ability.

Anyone putting Elizabeth's technique into action will see an immediate improvement in his or her singing – I and countless pupils of hers are proof positive that it works!

*Kathryn G. Harries FRAM ARAM B.MUS (hons) GRSM*
*Director of the National Opera Studio.*

4

# Introduction

First let me introduce myself. My first public performance was singing a little song written by my mother, herself a school teacher, pianist, singer and composer. I was four and a half years old, and the song ended on top A. We were having a musical evening in a hotel in Eastbourne. The manager refused to take any payment for my holiday!

After schooling at the Godolphin and Latymer School in Hammersmith, I entered the Royal Academy of Music at seventeen, continuing studies in Piano, Violin and Singing. I later added Viola and Organ, and graduated. After three years, I was appointed Sub-Professor of Singing, Aural Training and Rudiments. I then followed a career in Singing for twelve years, taking part in recitals in schools and music clubs, performing many times for the BBC in recitals, mostly of French Melodies, as well as singing as soloist in Oratorio with the BBC Chorus and Orchestra. I performed in Paris, Copenhagen, New York, and Ireland in Opera, Oratorio and recorded both for

L'oiseau Lyre in Paris and HMV. I spent one year in a review in the West End, with Joyce Grenfell, Max Adrian and Elizabeth Welsh as the stars.

I was invited to join the staff in the Junior Academy as Professor of Singing and Aural Training later, a post that I enjoyed for almost thirty years. In over seventy years of teaching Singing to males and females of all ages from 8 to 70+, I have come across so many keen pupils who just want to make music with the voice, but have many misconceptions as to what sounds they are producing, and perhaps a few hints may help them to achieve their desire.

*Elizabeth Cooper*

# Caution

It goes without saying that a fully trained singer is well-versed in elocution which means a study of articulation, breathing, vowel sounds, facial expression to suit the character of the material etc. It helps to acquire a sound knowledge of printed music, but many are quick to "pick up" a tune, and in choral singing that may be enough to start with. Try to watch the music as well as the words, and you will gradually make sense of it all. Since time immemorial, people have found singing as natural as breathing, and only want to improve the sounds they make. This little book might encourage those who like to sing in the bathroom where the resonance gives an enhanced sound to their voices, and would like to learn about getting more enjoyment out of singing. Choral singers especially sometimes have difficulties with their voices, and choir trainers are not always experts on singing technique!

Some people like to sing in the many competitive Festivals in Britain, and they will achieve higher marks if they learn some specific techniques which I hope I have covered in this book.

Before undertaking singing training, it should be understood that every time you open your mouth, whether to sing or to speak, you are using the only voice you have. Therefore think, before you shout or scream, because you may damage it irrevocably. Pop singers and music theatre actors please note! It is also worth noting that, just as smoke cures bacon or dries fish, if you smoke the same drastic changes may happen to your voice! We all know the gravelly voice of an inveterate smoker.

Those who decide to study singing seriously should note that it takes ten years to develop a voice to its full potential, both in tone quality and range; trying to hurry this process will only damage it. Ideally this training should not start until you are at least eighteen years old. That is not to say you cannot sing at all before then!

Common experience, so my doctor tells me, suggests that the voice is very resilient; so if yours has been

damaged, complete rest may bring it back to its former condition.

One famous soprano tried to sing in opera too early, and had to remain totally silent both in singing and speaking for a whole year!

The voice is a wind instrument located in the windpipe at the front of the neck. The so called vocal chords are really better described as two bits of "gristle" which vibrate when brought close together making a musical sound. The closer they are, the higher the sound produced. The natural range of an untrained voice is about nine notes; that is why most hymns and folk songs have a range of, at most, 10 notes. The trained voice can produce two octaves or more. Sopranos can develop to a range of up to three octaves in the case of a coloratura soprano.

# The Miracle

When a singer "thinks" the sound of each note, the vocal chords automatically adjust to make that exact pitch when the air passes between them. Not everyone has this miraculous gift, but the majority do. Some children only develop this by about the age of twelve. Those who do not are said to be "tone deaf". (I think this is a misnomer. Only if a person who cannot reproduce by whistling or singing a note that is in tune with one sung to them, or sounded on an instrument, deserves this description.) In my experience this cannot be rectified, and I advise learning to play an instrument - which is probably why instruments were invented in the first place as a substitute for the voice. The one that comes to mind first is the recorder. Incidentally, some elderly singers whose voices have deteriorated do try the recorder, and find this a wonderful hobby which affords some social activity with others. The Society of Recorder Players has branches in most areas, giving an opportunity to play any size of recorder in a recorder orchestra.

Music can be made using rhythms on drums, and some can be "tuned" to different pitches as in bongo drums, timpani, (or "kettledrums"), and the multi pitched steel drums. However, I return to my subject of making musical sounds with the voice, of which there are several categories.

# The Different Voices

The ranges of each voice can be found in the Appendix. It is not the range alone which determines which voice you have. Some very flexible ones can extend beyond the ranges suggested here. The qualities of each voice are described in the following passage.

### Coloratura Soprano
A light Soprano with a very high range. It is rare, but there are some operas which require such a voice, e.g. the Queen of the Night in Mozart's "The Magic Flute." The term "coloratura" also refers to very ornamented and fast passages for singers.

### Soprano, or Treble, usually applied to boys' voices.
The most normal high voice. There are: Dramatic Soprano, suitable for Wagner Opera, and Lyric Soprano which is the most versatile and is suitable for Mozart, Verdi, Puccini Opera, Lieder, Melodies (French songs, called Melodies, of Faure, Duparc, etc.) early opera and English song, and choral singing.

### Mezzo Soprano
A voice with rather richer tone than a soprano, and it does not usually have such a high range.

### Contralto
The lowest female voice, with rich tone. The quality of sound can be mistaken for a tenor.

### Counter Tenor, or Male Alto
A man who sings with the falsetto technique, which is achieved by only half the length of the vocal chords vibrating. Austrian singers of folk song often "yodel", which is achieved by alternating full voice with the falsetto. This is not recommended unless done very gently.

### Tenor
The high male voice. This range can be applied to Dramatic, or Heroic tenor, required in Wagner Operas, or Lyric Tenor, suitable for Lieder, French Melodies and English Song repertoire.

## Baritone

A Light Baritone voice sound very like a tenor in the upper register, but cannot quite reach the high A or B. It is not advisable for a light Baritone to try to take tenor roles if he wants to preserve his voice. This voice can be very useful in choirs, as her may be able to boost either the Tenors or Basses where the range is limited mainly to the middle of the gamut. The famous 19th Century singer, Jean de Reske, who had a Light Baritone voice, tried to pursue the tenor roles in Opera, but his voice was ruined after about ten years because of strain.

A Bass-Baritone should not try to emulate the richer tone of a true bass, nor try to extend his range to the very lowest notes required of a true Bass. This can cause a roughness in the quality of sound.

## Bass

The lowest male voice. Some singers, notably Russian basses. can sing a few notes lower than the usual range, even down to C-2.

# The Bellows

No, I don't mean Bellowing! All wind instruments operate by air passing through a tube-shaped object, as in recorders, flutes etc. and church organ pipes. The longer the pipe the deeper the pitch. (The organ in the Albert Hall has pipes for several different stops. For the lowest notes the pipes are each 32 feet long and simulate sound as of pipes 64 feet long feet long in one or two stops, for the very lowest note played by the pedals. (The "sound" of these is so low that it reverberates more like a deep "purr".) In the human, and all other living creatures that make sounds with the voice, a breath is taken in and the outgoing air passes through the "voice box" or larynx making a sound - a musical one if it is intended. Or speech (See The Miracle above.)

Training a voice cannot be done successfully until the student:
a) knows how his breathing works and….
b) practices breathing correctly at all times. This requires firstly, good deportment, standing tall, no hunching of shoulders and no tension in any part of the body, (excepting at certain moments detailed later).

# Breathing

When one asks a potential student "which is the effort, breathing in, or out?", nine out of ten will say "breathing in". This is usually because they tend to run out of breath on long notes or phrases, and tighten up the stomach muscles in their anxiety. This defeats the whole process.

If you have ever used a fire bellows, you will see that there is a valve, usually made of leather, covering loosely a hole through which air is sucked on opening the handles. As the air is pumped into the fire, the hole is covered again by the pressure inside the bellows. We have the same system, and here is a simplification to describe the process: If you hold a thin book - a slim music book is ideal, between your hands, pressure will cause the book to bend, (upwards to demonstrate this please), and then when the pressure is released the book falls level again. The book represents the diaphragm which lies between the thorax where the lungs are and the abdomen where the stomach and intestines are. Breathing then, is achieved by the rise

and fall of the diaphragm. The sternum is the bone running down the middle of the front of the chest from the collar bone to the seventh rib, and all these are fixed to it just as they are fixed to the spine at the back, making a cage for the vital heart and lungs. Below these are five so called "floating ribs", which are a little flexible and can be bent inwards by your hands pressing the sides of the chest. (You can feel the end of the sternum at the apex formed in the middle of the chest.) These therefore can be expanded by taking a really huge breath. However, the best way to expand them, and the essential way for singers, is by standing up straight, (see The Bellows) which raises the chest without the shoulders being raised (a teacher can demonstrate this by firstly standing badly, stooped a little, with the arms held out rather like two ribs, and then straightening up without changing the arm position at all at the shoulders, when it will be realised that the floating ribs, are raised automatically when the back is straightened, and the arms are raised up and out without using any arm muscles). This saves

the intake of breath a great deal of effort, as the major expansion has already been achieved. It is therefore only necessary to relax the stomach muscles while allowing the front of the chest to move forwards, and the breath is drawn in automatically. Of course, it is necessary to take in far more breath for singing in order to sustain long phrases in a melody than normal breathing. Normally one only takes deep breaths while running or exerting energy by such things as lifting heavy objects, because of the need for extra oxygen. Singing needs a lot of energy too!

There is another important aspect which should be observed. Nervousness can best be overcome by keeping as much air in your lungs as possible. There is a bad habit in many singers, who, at the end of a passage, leave it too late to breathe in deeply before the next phrase. Where there is a rest before your next entry, start taking a long slow breath, do not wait until just before you start singing. The intake of air should be quite silent. If there are several phrases

following each other quickly, "top up" as often as you can without distorting the phrasing or the sense of the words, to keep as full of air as possible all the time.

When teaching children and adults alike, it is most important that the mechanics of breathing are taught and repeated many times - and certainly at every lesson until the habit of correct breathing is acquired. Signs of tension are inevitable at first, as everyone feels vulnerable and self conscious. Encourage the desire to make musical sounds at all times.

A good trial is to sing far more than just "to the next breath mark", adding to the length of phrase each time of trying. Very soon, it will be possible to sing the whole of Baa, Baa Black Sheep in two breaths only. Then aim to sing the whole verse in one breath. However soft the tone, the proof is there that you have a far greater capacity that you think you have. For this exercise you need not worry about being loud, or putting in expression; it is simply a ploy to prove

to you that you have greater lungs that you think. It is never necessary to "push" the air out - just let the air out sparingly. There should be no change in the straight back, and anyone standing behind you should see no difference between when you are fully expanded with air and when you have used it all up. On a long phrase, aim to have used only half of the breath for the first ¾ of the phrase. You have used half when you realise your chest is about to shrink! This will allow you enough air to end the phrase well, even if there is a ritenuto or a pause at the end.

A series of very short notes sung on one pitch to the vowel "oo" with the lips rounded (in the shape for whistling) while using the diaphragm, (i.e. The front of the body just below the ribs will move in and out,) helps to strengthen this breathing muscle, as it is often called. Just as a violinist can achieve expression in his playing by the pressure of the bow on the string, the pressure of the air passing through the vocal chords allows a range of expression in singing, largely by control of the breath.

# Vowels

It is really important for you to have a vowel chart always to hand, (see Appendix) so that for the pure vowel sounds as well as the more unusual sounds in German and French, you can see what position the lips take and how wide the jaw should be opened to form these. The tongue plays a very important role in correct pronunciation.

As the study of different languages requires reference to the chart for correct vowels, the stumbling blocks as to French nasal vowels and mixed sounds, are soon overcome, even if the singer does not understand the language. That is not to say you do not need to understand the meaning of the words! Without knowing the sentiments in the poem you cannot adequately perform a song. Remember, singing is a double art - that of allowing the listener to appreciate the words as well as the music.

# The Teacher

It goes without saying that demonstrating by singing oneself is a great help in teaching the art, but some of my own teachers were men with tenor or bass voices, and well past their prime, while I was a soprano, and my first years of training were with Evelyn Langston of blessed memory, at the Royal Academy of Music in London. She herself was a coloratura soprano, but no longer a performer when I knew her.

Always ask if a pupil will mind being touched. It is necessary to do so when indicating which muscles keep the back straight, or explaining the working of the mouth, tongue, diaphragm etc. Despite the horror expressed by present -day "guidelines" about teachers touching pupils, I always explain that sometimes it is necessary when teaching singing or any musical instrument, to come into physical contact with a pupil, and where any parents object to this, I opt not to teach their child. In violin playing for instance, how is a pupil ever going to learn the correct position of

the hand and bowing arm, or how to hold the violin between the chin and the shoulder so that the left hand is free to use the fingerboard. (The uninitiated always suppose the left arm and hand hold the instrument up to the chin!)

# Resonance

What is meant by Resonance? If you hold a hand on your upper chest and speak, or sing very low notes, you will feel vibration under your hand. This means you are using the "chest voice", and the chest resounds for the lowest notes. Now place your hands on either side of your face, and sing a few notes which come easily without any reaching for high sounds. You will find the vibrating is now in your face and teeth. This range of notes is the middle register. The higher register resounds above the eyes, called the head voice, and in the coloratura range, notes above top C2 require the mouth to change to a smile, the resonance vibrating behind a line from ear to ear over the head. (I remember the first time I was able to sing "head notes" in a lesson, I felt quite dizzy with the vibration.)

Except for the highest coloratura notes, the mouth should always be well open, and the lips pushed forward; this forms an oval or oblong shape, with the corners of the mouth closer than in a relaxed position.

The front teeth should be clearly visible most of the time, with the lips forming a "trumpet". Until you have mastered the correct shape of the lips, do not try to smile as well. A smiling face while singing is often needed, but the lips must still make the "trumpet" shape. A smile is achieved as much with the eyes as the lips, while the cheeks will be tensed up a little. A smiling mouth alone is quite inexpressive! Your whole body is the instrument, and all of it resounds, just as the body of a cello enhances the volume of sound produced. Using a mirror, shape your mouth for the sound "u" (oo) - it should be small and round as in whistling. Now change to "i"(ee), but not relaxing the "oo" shape. The lips change to a small square shape. Keeping those lip muscles tense, half open the jaw for "e" as in "let", (the phonetic letter is like a 3 backwards, see vowel chart in Appendix)) and the mouth is shaped like a small oblong, then open the jaw fully and "uh" as in "up" will be produced, the mouth being a longer oblong shape. (This sound is the nearest to the Italian "a" in English. Until these shapes of the lips are really

mastered, you will not obtain the fullest and richest sounds with your voice. Only in the vowel "u" (oo) does the tongue leave the front lower teeth, because it becomes pointed and is positioned free of teeth or cheeks.

In the vowel "o" make sure you do not finish the sound with "oo" as the English speaker always does, as in saying "oh": neither should the sound be the English sound as in the word "hot".

# Belting

The less said about this the better. Let it be said that the popular music of today, especially in music theatre, encourages what is called Belting. This is when the speaking range of the voice, in other words the range of notes at the lowest sounds, which resound in the chest, are forced well above the natural area of resonance, producing harsh and ugly sounds; shouting in other words. Nobody hoping to be a singing artist in classical music, Grand Opera, choral or folk songs, should use this non-technique if they hope to retain a lovely sound throughout their lives. Belting will guarantee that after a few years the voice will sound harsh and unmusical. Indeed, the middle range of the voice will be destroyed by being constantly abused in this way.

# Diction

*A useful exercise for diction:*
Saying the letters of the alphabet followed by "ray" awakens the tongue as a good start, making sure you roll the "r" - thus: B-ray, B-ray, B-ray, BRAY, C-ray, C-ray, C-ray, CRAY, D-ray, D-ray, D-ray, DRAY and so on. Do not add a further vowel after the aspirated letters, (see Consonants.)

It is most important to have a mirror available when practicing. It should allow the singer to see his head and chest. Shaping the lips and tongue are not things we think about normally, and only by seeing what you are doing with them will enable you to learn what the various shapes feel like.

Vowel sounds are made by the tongue, combined with the position of the jaw, and a good exercise is widening and pointing this very flexible muscle. Imagine you have a bowl with some white powder in it, and you want to test whether it is sugar or salt. If you wet your finger and touch the powder, you don't want a large

amount on your tongue in case it is salt, so you point the tip of it to taste the powder at first. Sugar? Good! So you will then broaden the tongue to take a good lick! Seeing these movements in the mirror will enable you to control your tongue at will. For this exercise, do not allow the tongue to be touching the lips at all - keep it free in the middle of the mouth opening.

There is no vowel except "u", (the phonetic symbol pronounced "oo") where the tongue is not touching the lower front teeth, which avoids the tongue being pulled back, a common mistake, making quite the wrong sound. Too many people are afraid to show their tongues when speaking, leading to the mumbling of so many people you see on TV. Men are particularly prone to speak with their mouths almost shut. Close-up pictures of people singing sometimes show their tongues back in the mouth, giving a distorted vowel. Indeed, sometimes one could think they have no ability to open them at all! (have pity on deaf people who have to lip-read!) Elocution has not been a subject

taught in schools for decades, which has resulted in incorrect vowel sounds and very poor articulation of consonants not to mention leaving letters out altogether: dropping h's, using w instead of l, - as - "I don't feeoo weoo", and leaving off the "nt" in "don't".

The tongue must be at the front of the mouth, "washing" the backs of the lower front teeth for all the vowels except "u" as before mentioned.
The five pure vowels, *a, e, i, o, u,* which are the sounds used in Italian, have definite positions of the jaw and tongue; make the correct shape, and the correct sound will be heard. Some very slight changes can be heard when listening to a native Italian speaking, but for the purposes of singing they are not worth worrying about.
"a" should sound like the vowel in the word "cup", and not "ah". When this short sound is held longer, on a long note, it should not change to the English "ah" as in "are".
"e" … … … … … … .. "let"

"i" ............"beat"
"o" ............" boat" but without the sound "oo" at the end. This is quite hard to say if you are an English person, as this word uses a dipthong, two sounds, not a single pure vowel. You should always sing the greater part of the note on the first of the two vowels, except in "you, view, sue" etc. In those sing almost all the note on the second half of the diphong.
"u" ............"hoot".

These five sounds also occur in Russian and Italian, two of the best languages for learning to make the correct pronunciation of the five vowels.

In English there are nine dipthongs, "ei" (day), "au" (now) "ai" (my), "ou" (mow), "oi" (boy), "iu" (you), are some of them. There is another sound where the phonetic symbol is rather like an e upside down. This is the sound at the end of such a word as bitter, which, added to "i" comes in the word ear. Incidentally, for this sound you do not have to make any muscular shaping of lips, nor tongue, because

when these are totally relaxed, the sound is "er". So sometimes, if you are finding a phrase difficult, sing just the notes on this relaxed vowel, so that you are not "making" the vowel sound. A person who is almost unconscious will make this sound.

When singing a long note on a dipthong, you should sing almost the entire note on the first of the two sounds, except on "i" when the "i" comes quickly before the "oo", as in "you, few" the rest of the note staying on the second vowel. Pop singers almost always will sing the word "you" as YEE-U. This is because they have not addressed the problem presented by long notes sung on dipthongs. When singing a long note on a dipthong, never gradually change the second vowel during the note. Leave the tongue making the first sound, and just tuck the second vowel on at the last fraction of the note, except in "you" as mentioned above.

# Jaw and Lips

The shape of lips, and the three positions of the jaw, nearly closed, half-open and dropped completely, need careful attention if articulation is to be perfect for all languages. Symbols on your vowel chart (see Appendix) indicate these. If your speech is correct, you may already use them, but singing will exaggerate any wrongly produced sounds.

As the lips are very easily shaped, begin with looking in the mirror and form the vowel "u" (oo) with the lips pushed forward and almost closed, forming a small round hole, almost as small as that required to whistle. This should give the pure vowel which you would sing on the word "soon". Now, with all the same muscular shape held, try to say "i" (bee). The lips should remain pushed forward, but the lips form almost a square. The lips should be curled outwards away from the teeth; both upper and lower teeth should be seen when making this vowel. Now half-open the jaw, keeping the lips still pursed. This will be the correct shape for the vowel for which the phonetic letter is like a figure

three reversed, that is, facing to the right, (set, wet) then open the jaw fully, still showing the middle teeth, and the mouth becomes an elongated oblong vertically. This will shape the vowel (up), which is a short sound. Hold it longer, and it will give the Italian letter "a" as it is in cara. It should remain fully dropped. To sum up, all these shapes must be made in order to pronounce pure vowels: a, e, i, o, u.

Here are a few words using each of the five vowels.
"a" - but cut come rum sun.
"e" - bet set met men rent.
"i" - meet feat seat seal reel.
"o" There is no English word using this sound only. We always finish with "u", as in boat, coat, closing the lips with "u".
"u" root fool rule soon, (but not in some Northern local dialects as in foot, a shorter sound than "u")

# Consonants

Some consonants are made using the larynx (voice) and some are only aspirated, (made without using the larynx;) some come in pairs, so that the formation is the same, one using the voice, and the other aspirated.

*The pairs are:*
**B and P.** Whereas B must be sounded, P is made by using air that is in the mouth, in an explosive manner, but without air leaving the lungs. Bet, Pet.

**C and G** or **K and G**, are made at the back of the mouth by the soft palate touching the back of the tongue, without air leaving the lungs to make the sound: Cod, God. What is the soft palate? Well, if you run your tongue back along the roof of your mouth, the palate, it comes to a softer part; This is called the soft palate. In the middle of it there is a little bit hanging down called the uvula. This is what you flutter when speaking French, the gutteral "r": (not, however, when singing in French, because the soft palate needs to be manipulated for high notes.) In his book The

Interpretation of French Song, the renowned French singer Pierre Bernac emphasises this. (see also *High notes*.) (Look in the mirror, open your mouth and you can see the uvula hanging down at the back of your mouth.)

G is made the same way, but with air leaving the lungs, and the vocal chords vibrating.

**D and T**. D needs the voice to sound, whereas T only uses air in the mouth. Incidentally, if a word ending with D is followed by a vowel, the D is sounded normally. However, if it is followed by a consonant, T should be substituted for the D. e.g. "This and that" should be pronounced "this ant that." Otherwise we hear " this and-a that". Where a phrase ends on D as in God, it is necessary to pronounce an "upside-down" e to finish the word.

**F and V**. F is aspirated, and V uses the voice. e.g. ferry and very.

**J and CH**. J uses the voice, CH is aspirated. Chain, Jane.

**M, NG and N.** These are only hummed. How many tenors will open Handel"s Messiah with "Come-a fort-a ye"? There should not be any extra vowel here. Other arias comes to mind: "O rest in -a the Lord." These are done in the mistaken belief that only by finishing the word with a further syllable will the articulation be correct. However, if a phrase ends with the word "Lord", d being the last letter of the phrase, there should be a further sound, as Lorder, without the r of course, otherwise the last letter is lost altogether. "Come un - a -to him-a" is another frequently heard mistake: the individual syllables here do not need to be separated, and as the m is hummed there is no need to sing a further sound at the end of the note.

**R.** The rolled r is used during a word, but not at the end as in "butter", unless you wish to sound American.

**S and Z.** S is aspirated, and Z uses the voice. Seal zeal. The teacher must keep listening intently for any incorrectly made sounds, if pupils are to have good articulation.

# Trills

The technique involved to execute a trill is hardly ever correctly taught nowadays. The famous teacher, Garcia, in the mid nineteenth Century, set out a series of exercises for this ornament.

Most musicians recognise that a trill on a given note, say, C, will be a fluctuation between C and D or D flat. With the accent on the lower note. ***In singing, this is reversed.*** (see Appendix)

I always teach trills by firstly asking the pupil to sing D while I play the chord of C major. This requires a good ear and determination, as the voice will gravitate to C unless the singer is determined not to allow this. When a steady D is established, ask the singer to touch on a very short C immediately returning to the D again. Several single Cs sung separately in this way, then followed by two or three in a run, always focussed on singing D, will gradually allow for a longer trill. The rule is that you must keep ***thinking and pitching*** on the upper note, the lower note never really being "placed"

for even a split second. The voice remains steadily on D, and in fact the larynx "tips" a bit for every C. The larynx relaxes for a split second and returns to the original position . By putting your finger on the larynx you can do this manually. Watching a small bird trilling gives the clue. The throat vibrates during the trill.

It is fatal to start a trill by singing C-D-C-D a couple of times before trying to trill. Quite a few well- known sopranos and contraltos do this! This only establishes the sounds you *vainly* hope will then be heard as a trill. All that will be heard is a clumsy and doubtful note, not properly focussed on the pitch. Worse, some raise and lower the jaw to try and simulate a trill! The start must be in the rhythm - quaver - two semi quavers, The first being C and the two semi quavers being DC, thus continuing the trill with the accent on the upper note throughout. The trill exercise in the famous *Vaccai vocal exercises* demonstrates this perfectly.

# Performance

Singers should study the words of a song, and think about which actual letters will "paint" or convey the meaning clearly. Too often indistinct enunciation loses an opportunity to express the beauty of the lines. Singing is a double art - of conveying poetry and music together to the audience.

Expression is not only obeying the "hairpins", cresc., decresc. etc., and p and f in the score etc. There are many subtle ways in songs to add the individual touches which denote the true artist.

The most popular of Ralph Vaughan Williams' songs must be "Silent Noon", which is full of details which will enhance a performance. With a copy of this masterpiece before you, here are a few pointers about artistry.

**"Your hands lie open in the long fresh grass":** the word "long" will be enhanced if the hum on ng is held for at least a half of the note length. The sh of "fresh" gives extra colour to the word.

"The fingerpoints", this word is unusual, and needs almost slurred staccato notes (separated notes) to clarify the syllables: "your eyes smile peace": the z sound of eyes should be separate from the s in smile, but there is no need to take a breath, since z is made using the voice, while the s is only aspirated. Just stop after "eyes" and restart on "smile".

***"The pasture gleams and glooms 'neath billowing skies":*** The d of "and" needs to be t instead, otherwise there will be a unnecessary vowel inserted.

***"that scatter and amass":*** Do not roll the r of "scatter". A break between "scatter" and "and" will suffice.

***"All round our nest, far as the eye can pass":*** break between "nest" and "far" so that the st can be completed.

***"Are golden kingcup fields with silver edge":*** "kingcup fields", not everyone knows the name "kingcup", so this word needs very clear enunciation. Do not form a rolled r at the end of "silver".

***"where the cowparsley skirts the hawthorn hedge":*** Both of the h's should be sounded by using a small tightening of the diaphragm.

***"tis visible silence, still as the hourglass":*** This is a magical line - what an opportunity to paint the words here. Sung very softly and as in a straight line of sound, without moving the body in any way.

***"Deep in the sun searched growths":*** do not hurry, and take care not to make "growths" sound like "groves".

***"The dragonfly hangs":*** I think there should be a break at "hangs" (RVW possibly did not consider this.)
***"like a blue thread loosened from the sky":*** This part of the sentence is an adjectival phrase, and should not be interrupted by a breath. "loosened" needs a little longer on the ss to convey the meaning of the word.

***"so this winged hour is dropped to us from above":*** if a breath after "us" is taken, the next word, "from" should not be emphasised, but continue in the same tone.

***"Oh clasp we to our hearts, for deathless dower":*** A difficult line because "dower" is not a usual word. However, the word "clasp" is one which is dominated by the cl at the beginning. These letter should be a little separated. They give the sense of the word a greater emphasis.

***"This close companioned inarticulate hour":***
"Inarticulate" needs to be carefully enunciated.

***"When two fold silence was the song":*** Take a small breath after silence, when the palate should be raised, see "high notes", and the high "song" must be sung **with mouth wide open through the whole note, even after the ng is being held – but do not add another sound at the end.** This allows the beautiful effect of a decrescendo tailing off at the end of the note, in a hum. (I have heard so many quite good singers shut their mouths on the ng, which of course finishes the note suddenly and losing a great opportunity to paint the word.

"The song of love": In this repeated phrase, the "l" of "love" is the letter which paints the word, and on "song" a ***delicate*** portamento on the ng is effective. (slide the voice down after completing "song").

Applying some of the details suggested here to other songs will enhance your performances.

Do realise that when you know the notes and the words, you have now created a blank canvas on which you will then "paint" your own picture.

# High Notes

This applies to all voices, especially Sopranos and tenors, who tend to have more high notes to sing.

The soft palate needs to be raised in order to sing high notes without strain. You already do this every time you yawn. If you open the mouth widely you can induce a yawn quite easily. Indeed, it is possible to speak with the palate raised, but the sound of the voice will be distorted to a "wimpish" sound such as the famous actor Derek Nimmo used to good effect when he played roles such as a clergyman.

To sing a high note then, the palate must be raised. This can only be done when taking a breath. You cannot do it while actually singing. This means that, even if there are several notes to be sung prior to the highest note, they have to be sung with the palate raised also. A good tip is to breathe through the nose, which keeps the air warm and prevents a desire to cough, taking a short extra breath with the jaw fully

dropped, and then sing the passage immediately. This takes practice, giving yourself time before singing the phrase to do so. Practice makes perfect. Above all, do not be seen to make any extra effort to do this! By the way, did you know that you can open the jaw in two ways? If you place a pencil in front of your face, just touching the tip of your nose, and then drop your jaw, keeping the pencil at the same angle to the floor, the chin should recede a little. You can also open the jaw while keeping the chin touching the pencil, thus jutting the jaw forwards. This might make you feel and look belligerent and fierce, but it will cause tension in the jaw which is not required in singing at all.

In addition to having raised the soft palate, you must tense the buttocks and thighs when you reach the high note or notes (not however, the stomach). This gives support to the whole body which is your instrument, not just the voice box. Singing high notes can ruin the voice if not executed correctly. Singing in a choir when the composer asks the almost impossible, as in

Beethoven's Ninth Symphony, where sopranos sing high A for many bars, it is essential that every breath reinforces the raised palate, which can become tired. There should never be any feeling of aching or soreness in the throat after singing.

# Appendix

Avoid smoking, and a smoky atmosphere. Never shout or scream. Do not sing if you have any throat infection. However, a head cold can actually *increase* resonance for the first day or so. Eat a sensible diet. Get plenty of sleep especially just before an important singing engagement. Do not have a heavy meal for at least two or three hours before a performance. Drink plenty of water. A famous throat specialist who helps singers at the Middlesex Hospital in London, actually said to an audience of singers, "pee pale", in other words there should be almost colourless urine passed at all times. This helps the voice.

Treasure your gift of a good voice and never abuse it, and it should last all your life. If in old age it begins to lose its power, take up the recorder or some other wind instrument. I have had many elderly people delighted to come to recorder classes when they feel their singing days are numbered.

***The V represents how wide open the jaw is for each vowel***

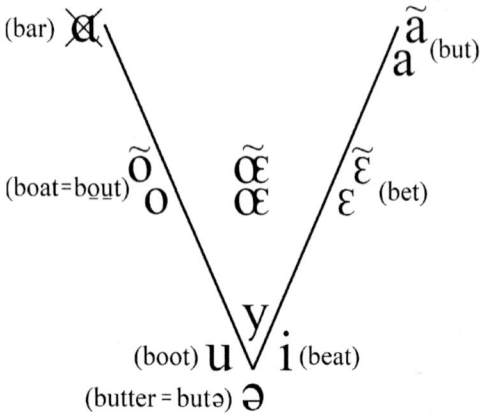

The letters with a tilde above indicate the four nasal sounds in the French language. There is no alternative way to pronounce these correctly without shaping the following positions of the mouth and tongue.

The basic four phonetic letters for these are - O, OE, A, E. The following examples may help you.

O with a tilde above as in "non, son", the mouth half open, the lips rounded, the air passing through the mouth and nose.

OE with a tilde above, This requires three different

positions. The mouth as for O, the tongue as for e as in let, met, and then pronounced nasally. This occurs in "un, brun, chacun".

A with a tilde above, as in "mange, chant" (without pronouncing the t at the end), or en as in "enfant" which in phonetics is simply the same phonetic letter with f between. Both en and an use the same phonetic letter.

E with a tilde. The mouth half open, as in "let", and then pronounced nasally. In French this is the vowel for "in, ein," as in fin, main. Some words use two of these nasal vowels such as enfin, enfant.

Unless these sounds are practiced, English speakers sometimes neglect the correct jaw, tongue and lip positions which gives a clue as to the original speech of the singer! There are no short cuts. In such words as "enfant, enfin" there is no letter n sounded at all. OE requires the mouth as for O, and the tongue as for

E, as in heureuse, fleur. For the nasal sound you will be saying un, parfun, chacun. all of these sounds must be spoken and practiced frequently so that the formation of the mouth and tongue are always correct.

I hope that this little book will help you to sing really well, without getting hoarse after a choir rehearsal, or after your daily practice.

Coughs and colds are such a nuisance for singers, but the early stages of a head cold can, for a day or so, enhance the resonance. Indeed, I once sang a Bach aria in a broadcast, with a head cold. There was no difficulty, and no one present had an inkling of my little problem.

In the Royal Academy of Music there used to be a mosaic in the floor with the words **"Sing unto God"**. This has always inspired me in my work, and although I can no longer sing as I did, I expect to sing in the life to come!